THIS HISTORIC GROUND

NOTRE DAME STADIUM
1930—1997

Special thanks to Linda Dunn, Notre Dame Photographic Department; Charles Lamb and Matthew Steffens, University Archives; Victoria Van Patten; Bill Steinmetz; Chuck Lennon and Karen Anthony, Notre Dame Alumni Association; Dennis K. Moore, Public Relations and Information; Bruce Harlan; Mike and Sue Bennett; John Heisler and Mike Enright, Notre Dame Sports Information; Kent Stevens, College Football Hall of Fame; Chris Broadhurst; Sr. Kathleen Beatty; Jeff Cerney and Tim Conley, Casteel Construction Corp.; and Ray Mann.

This book is dedicated to my husband, Don Hall, to my parents, Bob and Jan Blazi, and to all other Notre Dame football fans around the world.—TH

GOLDEN LEGACY — *Terry Meyer of Conrad Schmitt Studios, New Berlin, WI, applies gold leaf to the etched stone above the north entrance to Notre Dame Stadium. It is the same gold as used on the famed golden dome atop the University's historic Main Building.*

THIS HISTORIC
GROUND

NOTRE DAME STADIUM
1930—1997

TEXT BY TERRI HALL '80

EDITED BY JAIME OWEN CRIPE '89

LAYOUT BY DWIGHT LUNA

CONCEPT AND PHOTOGRAPHS BY
KEVIN BURKE

© 1997 by Ave Maria Press, Inc.

International Standard Book Number: 0-87793-636-6

Library of Congress Catalog Card Number: 97-69935

Printed and bound in the United States of America.

"I WISH I COULD PROMISE YOU A NATIONAL CHAMPIONSHIP THIS COMING SEASON AND EVERY SEASON THEREAFTER, BUT WE KNOW ALL TOO WELL: THAT'S NOT THE WAY THE GAME WORKS. THIS I CAN PROMISE YOU: STARTING THIS SEASON, TWENTY THOUSAND MORE FIGHTING IRISH FANS WILL BE SHAKING DOWN THE THUNDER, AND MORE THAN EVER, **THIS HISTORIC GROUND** WILL BE A RALLYING POINT FOR WHAT COUNTS MORE THAN ALL THE NATIONAL CHAMPIONSHIPS PUT TOGETHER: THE SPIRIT OF NOTRE DAME."

—BOB DAVIE, HEAD FOOTBALL COACH
AT THE UNIVERSITY OF NOTRE DAME, 1997

The spirit of Notre Dame...the tradition, devotion, courage, and commitment to excel-lence...is the reason why the original Notre Dame Stadium was built and, finally, renovated and expanded nearly seven decades later.

Built in 1930 in an Indiana farm field by a small, religious men's college, the stadium had seats for nearly 60,000 football fans—20 times the University's enrollment of the day. At the start of the Great Depression, its construction employed as many as 500 men and, like another of the principal landmarks on campus—the golden domed Main Building—required less than five months to complete. It cost $800,000.

The price tag for the recent renovation was $50 million and it took nearly two years to complete. "The House That Rockne Built" now allows seating for 80,225 fans, an increase from the original and well quoted 59,075. One reason the renovation took as long as it did to finish is that construction was hampered in 1996 as Notre Dame continued to play its home games in the stadium. In 1929, during the original construction, the Irish played their "home" games in Chicago's Soldier Field.

In the 67 years since its opening, Notre Dame Stadium has come to mean so much to so many—referred to at various times as the "House That Rockne Built," Home of the Heisman (a record seven Heisman Trophy winners have played for Notre Dame), and the Cradle of Champions (an unprecedented 11 national titles).

This book preserves the history of the stadium and explains why a small, midwestern liberal arts college needed such an elaborate sporting field in the first place; the ploy legendary Irish football coach Knute Rockne used when the University told him "no stadium," and how it almost backfired; the origins of some of the stadium's unique traditions; and the legacy of Notre Dame Stadium on the field and in the stands.

In the words of people connected to the stadium during its lifetime and the stories they tell, you'll discover that Notre Dame Stadium is more than just America's best known stage for college football. It is HISTORIC GROUND.

1

When word came that Notre Dame was going to build a football stadium, architectural and construction bids arrived on campus from across the country. Ultimately, the Osborn Engineering Company of Cleveland, Ohio, was chosen to design the structure. The company had experience through the layout and construction of stadia at the Universities of Michigan and Indiana and Purdue University, as well as Chicago's Comiskey Park, and New York's Yankee Stadium— "The House That Ruth Built," to this day one of the few other American sports venues with a lore as long and rich as Notre Dame Stadium. But, while "the Bambino" would play 13 seasons in the house he built, "Rock" would see only one (five games) in his.

Rockne was an educated man in ways other than football. He graduated magna cum laude from Notre Dame in 1914 and was asked to stay on as a chemistry instructor, as well as to assist then-football coach Jesse Harper. Rockne's input established the basic design of the 59,000-seat Notre Dame Stadium: a scaled-down version of the University of Michigan's enormous, 101,000-seat bowl in Ann Arbor. Prior to Notre Dame Stadium, the football team played at Cartier Field. It was torn down in the spring of 1929, and the squad used Soldier Field in Chicago as its home field for the '29 season.

The *South Bend Tribune* reported in jest that Rockne wanted the stands at Cartier torn down quickly so the University could not change its plans. He might have been

more right than he realized, as the team had its worst season under Rockne in 1928 with five wins and four losses. Things picked up, however, in 1929 and '30, when the teams went undefeated and were national champions.

Ground was broken for the new stadium in September 1929. However, construction did not begin until April 1930. The new campus landmark was completed in only four months by construction crews that came from all over the United States. They were supervised by Ralph Sollitt and Sons of South Bend, general contractors for the project.

In October 1929, the *Notre Dame Scholastic* reported that "numerous small buildings which house the tools and equipment sheds, lumber racks, and the field offices of the contractor and the engineers" already were popping up near the construction site. Raising the stadium took a workforce of 500 men, who reportedly ate a ton of food a day. Each worker also drank more than a gallon of water each day.

An article in the *Notre Dame Alumnus* said that 45,000 cubic feet of earth was moved for the grading and foundations of the new stadium. All of the materials needed to build the arena were brought in by train. They included 75 freight carloads of cement; 29 carloads of Indiana limestone for the exterior; 20 carloads of steel weighing more than 400 tons; and about 500 carloads of sand and gravel. Two million bricks were used in the construction.

1. October 22, 1921: The Notre Dame Ramblers (as they were nicknamed at the time) are shown defeating Nebraska (7-0) during the Homecoming game at Cartier Field. Notre Dame football teams played all their home games there in the 1920s, and in 1927 changed their nickname to "The Fighting Irish."

2. October 8, 1929: Ground-breaking and layout for Notre Dame Stadium. The Notre Dame Alumnus *reported that 45,000 cubic feet of earth was moved for the grading and foundations of the new stadium.*

3. May 25, 1930: The sod is laid for the football field. A patch from the old Cartier Field also is used to preserve the winning tradition in the new stadium. Coach Rockne declares the arena will be used exclusively for football.

2

3

The *South Bend Tribune* noted that "much of that excavation of 15-feet of earth below field level was completed with the use of horses pulling drag shovels. Steam shovels and trucks were also used. Another phase of construction also seemed unusual. Completed concrete sections of the stadium were formed outside the perimeter of the stadium and then moved into place before the 100,000 feet of redwood seating was installed."

One University student at the time, James Carmody, worked out some interesting facts and figures regarding the construction items for the new stadium. These calculations were published in the *Official Football Review* of 1930. This "statistician extraordinaire" estimated that:

"...if the 2 million bricks were laid end to end they would reach from the Administration Building to the Cleveland waterfront, or a matter of some three hundred miles..."

"...if we take only the steel that makes up the framework of the stadium...there were 400 tons of it used, or more simply, 20 carloads. Let us make bullets of it and there will be 6,400,000 of them, if two ounces were used for each one. If they were fed steadily into a machine gun which shoots one hundred of them a minute, the trigger would be pressed for 44 days and ten hours before the supply would be exhausted."

"...if a table were to be made of the 100,000 feet of California redwood lumber used for the seats...if it were four feet wide, it would stretch for a distance of 25,000 feet. And 20,000 people could be accommodated for meals at one time."

4. May 10, 1930: *Stands are going up and the "tunnel" is taking shape. The stadium's construction required a workforce of 500—men fortunate to have work just seven months after the Crash of '29, the start of the Great Depression.*

5. *Construction begins on the new stadium. Notice the Golden Dome in the upper left corner. Carloads of construction materials are spread out and ready to go. Small buildings are set up to house tools and equipment. Also visible are the field offices of the contractor (Ralph Sollitt & Sons, South Bend, Indiana) and engineers and architects (Osborn Engineering Company of Cleveland, Ohio).*

6. *Concrete is poured into forms making up 60 rows spaced just 24 inches apart. While keeping fans close to the action on the field, watching from these seats can sometimes be an even more "intimate" experience. More than 100,000 linear feet of California redwood seating—selected for its durability—was installed in the original stadium. Each spectator gets 11 inches.*

ootball began at Notre Dame in 1887. By 1899, when Knute Rockne was 11 years old, interest in the sport was sufficient that Cartier Field was erected just north of the current stadium where the University's Decio Faculty Hall stands today. However, the gridiron's grandstands held fewer than 30,000 fans, not enough with the boom in popularity of Notre Dame's football program during the "Roaring '20s." As a result, Knute Rockne—who graduated from Notre Dame in 1914 and was named head football coach in 1918—rallied ND alumni and football fans across the country in a crusade for a new football venue. And Rockne used more than his coach's whistle to gain attention for his cause.

Rockne wrote letters to business owners in South Bend asking them to purchase season tickets at $5 each so that University officials could see the growing support for the team. Albert Erskine, head of South Bend's Studebaker Automobile Corporation, responded by ordering 100 tickets. Other orders soon followed. It was reported, too, that Rockne walked the streets of South Bend placing tickets at lunch counters, cigar shops, and newsstands.

DEDICATION NOTRE DAME STADIUM
NAVY vs NOTRE DAME
OCTOBER 11, 1930 50¢
OFFICIAL PROGRAM

Ransom message demands beer in return for stolen Rockne bust

By MARGARET FOSMOE and JEFF HARRINGTON
News Editors

Richard Conklin.

A major investigation has not been launched into the case of the kidnapped coach, although

but he's not talking either.

The Sorin statue has been the victim of several abductions

The missing Knute Rockne statue from the lobby of Memorial is resting comfortably on a Florida beach ransom note that accompanied this photograph.

Rockne visits the Hoosier Dome

By MARGARET FOSMOE
Executive Editor

The stolen bronze bust of Knute Rockne made the trip to the Hoosier Dome last weekend, according to a note delivered yesterday to *The Observer* office.

Accompanying the note were several photos displaying the bust of the famous Notre Dame football coach. The figure was dressed in a in a Purdue University jersey. *(See photos at right.)*

The note was the first information received by *The Observer*

the University regulation in *Du Lac* concerning premarital sex.

The statue, approximately two feet tall and two feet broad at the base, disappeared from its pedestal in Rockne Memorial on May 5.

One photo shows the bust posed outdoors in front of a road sign marked "Welcome to West Lafayette, Purdue University."

The other two photos display the bust seated indoors at a table. In one, two arms from behind the statue grasp an axe on the table while a voice balloon above the figure contains the words "Where's Gerry?" In the third, two arms reach around the figure for an unidentified object on a plate.

Notre Dame Security has received information concerning the stolen bust, according to Assistant Director of Security Rex who received some information forwarded to the Police Department supposed to lead."

ward Sorin located in Sorin Hall,

Rakow refused to tell what the information was, saying only "It involves some people on campus."

On May 18, a single photo of the bust accompanied a ransom note that was delivered to *The Observer* office. That note alluded to the new alcohol policy and indicated that the bust would not be returned "till the students have their beer." It was addressed to "Father Ted" and signed "Rock."

A photograph accompanying the May note showed the bust, in sunglasses, sunning on a beach surrounded by a beer keg, a portable stereo and a frisbee.

The Rockne figure was taken last spring after articles in *The Observer, Notre Dame Magazine,* and the *South Bend Tribune* described the history of the Father Sorin statue located in Sorin Hall. The Sorin statue was the victim of several abductions during the past 30 years.

Knute Rockne apparently made a visit to Indianapolis recently as these photos, sent anonymously to The Observer, show.

WELCOME TO
Wes Lafayette
Purdue University

1. This bust of Rockne can be seen in two places on campus: the Joyce Center and the Rockne Memorial. Legend says it is good luck to rub Rockne's nose. In 1984, the Memorial's bust of Rockne was "kidnapped" by some students and taken on a cross country trek. The campus newspaper, The Observer, ran stories and photographs of Rock on a beach in Florida and at Purdue University. The bust was returned to its Notre Dame home during a student rally.

2. Knute Rockne in an advertisement for the Studebaker Automobile Corporation. In addition to his coaching duties, Rockne was sales promotion director for the Studebaker Corporation headquartered in South Bend. He reportedly received $10,000 for six motivational speeches given to the carmaker's sales staff.

ratulations from a Champion to a Champion

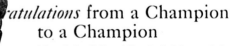

tre Dame and Knute Rockne, Builders of Champion football teams, Stude-
r, Builder of Champion motor cars, extends congratulations. Your magnifi-
adium is a reward well won. It is as much a symbol of courage and sportsman-
s the Gold and Blue itself. It is a credit to the University, and to South Bend, as
May it echo often to the triumphant strains of "The Victory March"!

TUDEBAKER
Builders of Champions

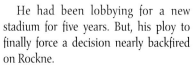
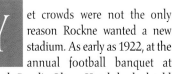

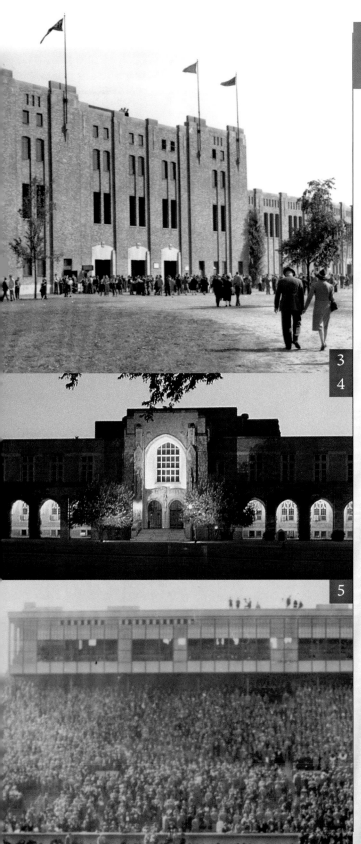

Yet crowds were not the only reason Rockne wanted a new stadium. As early as 1922, at the annual football banquet at South Bend's Oliver Hotel, he had told the crowd that the Notre Dame team could not expect to attract major opponents to the city unless a larger facility were approved. South Bend's mayor, Franklin R. Carson, reportedly answered Rockne with a promise that a committee would look into the matter.

Nothing came of that pledge, however, and in 1924—after winning the national championship—Rockne felt the time was right to address the issue again. This time, University officials informed the coach that a new stadium could not be considered for at least five years, until new residence halls and academic buildings were constructed for the growing number of students on campus. (This was more or less the same reasoning used by the University in deferring a decision to expand the stadium during the sell-out decades of the 1970s and '80s. During that time, Notre Dame went fully coeducational, putting unique pressures on the University for new residential and classroom facilities required by a larger and more diverse student body.) But once those buildings were completed, Rockne renewed his fight for a bigger stadium in earnest. After the 1927 season, when he still had extracted no firm commitment from the University for a new stadium, Rockne grew more and more frustrated. He submitted his resignation to then-Notre Dame President Rev. Matthew Walsh, CSC:

Dear Father,

You will pardon the appearing formality of this note, but I wish to hereby tender my resignation to you as Head Coach and would appreciate your accepting at your convenience.
Yours very sincerely,
KK Rockne.
November 27, 1927

He had been lobbying for a new stadium for five years. But, his ploy to finally force a decision nearly backfired on Rockne.

In its logical consideration, the administration felt that the Notre Dame football team would not be as successful without Rockne. So if he resigned, there was no need for a new stadium. After some discussion, the administration decided that Rockne would stay on as head coach and athletic director and committees would be set up to conduct a feasibility study on the construction of a new stadium.

Still, things did not move quickly enough for Rockne. In 1928, he again threatened to resign, and this time he had better luck. Now, even the new president of the University, Rev. Charles O'Donnell, CSC, was feeling pressure from alumni and fans for tickets. He vented his frustration at the 1929 football banquet:

"These somewhat premature gray hairs of mine, gentlemen, are not due to worries over insufficient endowment, or to the inadequate facilities of our physical plant, or to any one of a number of matters. No, it's the unusual beating which all of us to some degree...must take in this matter of football ticket demands."

At last, the go-ahead came. Rockne insisted that the field be used only for football. He preferred the curved stands he saw at the University of Michigan. The curves were then a new idea, allowing more seats "between the goal posts," that is, along the sidelines, than other designs of the time.

Neither did Rockne want a track between the stands and the field as was the custom in other stadia. Instead, the concourse of the stadium originally was filled with cinder, and the track team used the area to practice. Stadium personnel had to rake out the cinders after each football game to remove cigarette and cigar butts, as well as the trash that fans left behind.

3. Fans entering the newly-built stadium outside Gate 14 on the west side of the building. During the 1995-97 renovation, Gate 14 was closed up and the space converted to a concession stand.

4. The Rockne Memorial Building was erected in 1937 to honor the great football coach. Among its facilities are gymnasia, a swimming pool and weight rooms, plus handball and racquetball courts. The football staff's offices were located there until the Joyce Center opened in 1968.

5. The stadium during a game in 1930. Notice the team dugouts. They were removed during the 1950s.

1. The ticket office also housed the hats for the stadium's ushers. More than 800 men worked as ushers at each home game until 1996 when the first woman—Cheryl Floyd of Osceola, IN—became an usher.

2. 1931: A crowd of football fans outside the new stadium. A souvenir stand is set up for business (right-center of the photograph).

3. The concourse on the west side of the stadium inside Gate 14. The Fighting Irish track team formerly used the old concourse—nearly a half mile in circumference—for practice.

CARNEGIE TECH vs NOTRE DAME

OFFICIAL PROGRAM
October 20, 1934
NOTRE DAME STADIUM

25¢
NOVEMBER 23, 1935

SO. CALIFORNIA NOTRE DAME

NOTRE DAME STADIUM

OFFICIAL PROG

DRAKE

OCTOBER

NOTRE DAME STADIUM   OCTOBER 2 · 1937

SEC. 27

SEC. 26

In 1930, Notre Dame Stadium was unique for several reasons. The *Notre Dame Alumnus* reported: "The curved stand, a new idea in stadium construction, gives the maximum amount of seats between the goal posts. It also faces everybody toward the center of the field rather than at right angles to it, as in the case of other rectangular stands." Five hundred boxes along the sidelines on both sides of the field were sold to pay most of the cost of construction. Each box held six chairs; prices ranged from $1250 to $3000 depending on the box's proximity to the 50-yard line. With each purchase, the title of the box would remain in the buyers' names for ten years, during which time they also had the chance to buy the best seats for Notre Dame's road games.

Since most of the box seats were paid for in advance, work on the stadium continued after the stock market crash of 1929. Rockne kept a close eye on the progress. He even supervised the parking and traffic system around the stadium.

Regular tickets for the 1930 season were sold for $3 and reserve seats were $5. For the stadium dedication game against Navy, the top price was increased to $7.

The University had fewer than 3000 students in 1930, but its legions of football fans went far beyond that. Arriving spectators entered through any of 18 gates and could quickly get into their seats via sloping ramps leading to 36 portals in the original bowl. And if for some reason the stadium had to be emptied quickly, it was estimated that it could be accomplished in about fifteen minutes. Each team had a dugout enclosed on three sides to protect it from the South Bend weather. These dugouts were well below the first row seats so no one's view was blocked. They were removed sometime during the 1950s. During the stadium's recent expansion, the first two seating rows and most of the "field" seats were removed (except those for the band). As a result, that "on top of the action" feeling may be lost to many fans.

4. The box seats area behind the home team dugout featured the stadium's famous—or infamous—green folding chairs, many of which were purchased by fans and collectors. The chairs have been replaced with fixed seating.

5. The concession stands have been a favorite at Notre Dame Stadium since it opened. Among the most obvious changes over the years is the list of prices. Coffee, soft drinks, and hot dogs all sold for a dime. Ham sandwiches were 20 cents. And cigars and cigarettes were still sold. The University banned smoking in the stadium in 1994.

6. The parking lots have been jammed since the stadium opened. However, there's not a tailgate party in sight.

7. Not a seat to be had in the house! An aerial view of the stadium in 1941, when Frank Leahy began his coaching career at Notre Dame.

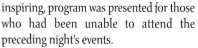

The first game played in the new stadium was against Southern Methodist University. About 15,000 fans attended and saw the Irish win 20-14. The stadium's "Dedication Game" was played a week later, on October 11, 1930, against Navy. More than 40,000 fans joined in the festivities. At sunset the night before the game, the cheerleaders and the band led a parade of students and supporters toward the new campus landmark. The procession started at Lyons Hall and went from dormitory to dormitory picking up other members of the student body as it continued through campus. Off-campus students assembled at the fire station on Notre Dame Avenue and joined the marching mass at the post office. The line was reportedly three blocks long. Some students carried flaming torches, and the crowd sang out the "Victory March." There were other songs and fireworks, too, for the celebration. More than 100 airbombs were set off to announce the history-making event at Notre Dame.

Just prior to the football game the next day, a shorter, yet still inspiring, program was presented for those who had been unable to attend the preceding night's events.

Wondering about the score of the game? The Irish won 26-2.

"The sod that carpets the floor of this stadium is rich in traditions. For a quarter of a century, athletes who have added to the fame of Notre Dame have raced over its emerald surface carrying our colors to victory, or have opposed with their bodies charging opponents seeking the coveted goal line."

—Frank Hering, captain of the 1896 team and then-president of the Notre Dame Alumni Association, in a speech at the dedication ceremonies for Notre Dame Stadium. Hering also is credited with suggesting in 1904 that a day be set aside each year to honor mothers…a suggestion that later officially became Mothers' Day.

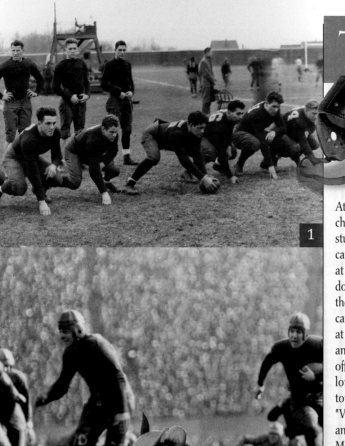

1. The Irish practice for the first game in their new home: Notre Dame Stadium. The practice paid off. Notre Dame was undefeated in 1930.

2. Scene from the stadium dedication game vs. Navy. The Irish sank the Middies, 26-2.

3. Although 40,000 fans turned out to see this matchup between the Irish and Navy, it was not a sellout. The first sellout was in 1931 when the Trojans of the University of Southern California came to South Bend. A field goal in the final minutes of the game gave the victory to USC, 16-14. It was the first time the Irish had lost since 1928. With the exception of a Thanksgiving Day game in 1973, every Notre Dame home game since 1966 has been sold out. Even with 20,000 new seats created by the '95-'97 renovation, no Notre Dame football tickets are offered for sale to the general public.

4. October 11, 1930: Souvenirs from the stadium's dedication game included this Navy goat, the mascot of the Midshipmen then and today.

5. Notre Dame's mascot was not always the famous Leprechaun of today. That place in history belongs to "Clashmore Mike," an Irish terrier. A first terrier—actually named Brick Top Shuan-Rhu—was given to Knute Rockne by Charles Otis of Cleveland, Ohio, prior to a game in 1930. Taking that cue, class of 1919 alum Arthur Christian Weinrich helped establish the dog as the school's first official mascot, supplying the Irish terriers as needed for many years.

Notre Dame, Our Mother, tender, strong and true,

Proudly in the heavens gleams thy Gold and Blue.

Glory's mantle cloaks thee, golden is thy fame,

And our hearts forever praise thee, Notre Dame.

And our hearts forever love thee, Notre Dame.

Notre Dame's Alma Mater, "Notre Dame, Our Mother," was debuted at the stadium's dedication. Written by Joseph J. Casasanta, a 1923 graduate of the University, this tribute to the Blessed Virgin Mary continues to be played by the Band of the Fighting Irish at the conclusion of every game in Notre Dame Stadium.

The Irish went undefeated that debut season for Notre Dame Stadium and were named national champions. Rockne never lost a game there. But his first season in Notre Dame Stadium would also be his last. On March 31, 1931, he boarded an airplane for a trip to Los Angeles. He was to assist in the production of the movie "The Spirit of Notre Dame," starring Lew Ayres. Shortly after taking off, the plane flew into a storm and became covered with ice. It crashed into a wheat field near Bazaar, Kansas, and there were no survivors. Rockne was 43.

Since Rockne did not want the stadium named for him, the University built another athletic facility and dedicated it in his memory. The Rockne Memorial Building is located at the west end of South Quad and is affectionately known as "The Rock."

Fans across the country mourned Rockne's death. However, their interest in Notre Dame football never waned, and it wasn't long before the new stadium was sold out. In fact, every seat was filled when the University of Southern California came to play on December 6, 1931. The game was for the national championship, and the media called it the "Clash of the Colossi." In the final minutes, USC kicked a field goal to win 16-14. It was the first time the Irish had been beaten since 1928. Fans, stunned by the loss, remained in their seats in disbelief. Rockne had spoiled them. Almost immediately, they started calling for the resignation of Hunk Anderson, Rockne's successor. It would be five years before the stadium was sold out again.

6. For 67 years, game days inside Notre Dame Stadium looked just like this: the Fighting Irish playing to a full house in the autumn sunshine on natural turf. This view from the early '60s shows the Memorial (now Hesburgh) Library prior to the "Word of Life" mural's addition to the south facade in 1964.

7. A work of art as famous as any in the world to Irish fans, the "Word of Life" mosaic is more casually known on campus as "Touchdown Jesus."

8. A Notre Dame sweater (c. 1930s) that can be seen in the concourse at the Joyce Center among many other sports artifacts on display.

1. The rivalry with Navy is the longest in Notre Dame history—spanning 70 games since 1927—and among the longest in all of college football. On this scoreboard, (c.1950) only the game clock runs electrically.

2. A behind-the-scenes look; before electronic scoreboards were installed, the scores were posted manually. Sometimes the students changing the numbers had to work hard to keep up. In 1944, Notre Dame beat Dartmouth (64-0) and then Pittsburgh (58-0) by a combined score of 122-0.

1   2

NOTRE DAME 31 **0:00** FLORIDA ST 24

TIME OUTS LEFT — QTR. — TIME OUTS LEFT

DOWN — TO GO — BALL ON

"WHEN THIS YEAR'S TEAM BEGAN THE SEASON IN THE NEW STADIUM IT WAS TOLD, IN EFFECT,

'YOU ARE GIVEN THIS SOD UPON WHICH TO PLAY, BUT WITH IT YOU ARE GIVEN A RESPONSIBILITY. YOU ARE MADE CUSTODIANS OF NOTRE DAME'S TRADITION OF VICTORY.'

THE SCORE CARDS SHOW HOW THE TEAM HAS CARRIED ON THAT TRADITION."

–Arch Ward, Sports Editor of the Chicago Tribune in a 1930 Notre Dame Football Review article entitled "And Something Abides"

3. A moment to remember: the 1993 Notre Dame-Florida State game—the battle for No. 1, billed as the "Game of the Century." With three seconds left in the game and time for just one Florida State play, Irish cornerback Shawn Wooden knocked down a pass in the end zone to preserve Notre Dame's 7-point win.

4. Behind the scenes (1993) of the electronic scoreboards: Notre Dame's Video Systems crew tapes the Irish games for review the next day.

5. Needed for the 1996 season, the brick scoreboard towers were among the last pieces of the original stadium to be removed as part of the structure's renovation and expansion.

SECTION TWO:
"HALLOWED GROUND"

Notre Dame began as a small, midwestern school for boys, but it has evolved into a University recognized worldwide for both its academic excellence and the achievements of its athletes, male and female. It's been said that God must love Notre Dame fans because he made so many of them.

Presidents, movie stars, and many others of national and international prominence have visited the University and attended a football game during their stay. Among them were President John F. Kennedy and his wife, Jackie. In 1961, Kennedy was awarded Notre Dame's Laetare Medal, the University's highest honor recognizing outstanding Catholics in America.

Another luminary was Patriot of the Year award winner comedian Bob Hope, known for his many USO tours to entertain American servicemen overseas, as well as the classic series of "Road Pictures" with Bing Crosby and Dorothy Lamour. There was no "Road to Notre Dame," however.

On December 6, 1930, the first season for the new stadium, humorist Will Rogers was in the stands. The Irish were playing a team that was described as "unbeatable"... the Trojans of USC. Rogers, nicknamed "the cowboy philosopher," described the game:

"There we were all packed in the stadium, really pitying those poor little boys from back there in South Bend and hoping that the California kids wouldn't seriously hurt any of them running over them on the way to the goal posts. Well, on the very first play USC fumbled. From then on it was just too bad. You never saw a team beaten so coolly and deliberate-like. Notre Dame was a machine doing things where the others were trying to with their hands."

The game was a shutout. The Irish won 27-0.

Still another visitor was writer James Michener—author of the 1947 Pulitzer Prize-winning *Tales of the South Pacific*—who praised Notre Dame Stadium in his book *Sports in America*:

"To attend a game at Notre Dame and to watch the medieval mania that settles upon the institution as game time approaches is to see football at its best."

1. President John F. Kennedy enjoys a 1961 Notre Dame game in the company of his wife, Jackie (right), and sister, Eunice. JFK was on campus to receive the University's Laetare Medal. Eunice Kennedy Shriver would connect with Notre Dame 26 years later (see opposite page) as founder of Special Olympics.

2. President Richard Nixon and his wife, Pat, also attended an Irish football game. In 1960, then-Vice President Nixon was given the Patriot of the Year Award by Notre Dame's senior class for his diplomatic work in South America and the Soviet Union.

3. Academy Award-winning actress/comedienne Irene Dunne is shown in the stadium in 1949. Dunne starred in movies including "The Awful Truth," "Cimarron," and "Theodora Goes Wild," as well as appeared on television's "Ford Theatre" and "The Loretta Young Show." She's on the right in front of future University President Rev. Theodore Hesburgh, CSC, and sitting next to Mr. and Mrs. Howard Phalin. The Phalins donated the "Word of Life" mural on the Memorial Library.

4. Democratic Presidential nominee, Sen. Adlai Stevenson, chats with an Eisenhower backer in this shot from the stadium. For an unexplained reason, the woman's lapel button is in French.

5. New York City Mayor "Gentleman" Jimmy Walker (first row, second from right in white hat) visited Notre Dame Stadium during its first year.

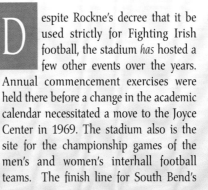

Despite Rockne's decree that it be used strictly for Fighting Irish football, the stadium *has* hosted a few other events over the years. Annual commencement exercises were held there before a change in the academic calendar necessitated a move to the Joyce Center in 1969. The stadium also is the site for the championship games of the men's and women's interhall football teams. The finish line for South Bend's Sunburst marathon has been the stadium's 50-yard line.

In 1987, the International Summer Special Olympics Games were held at Notre Dame and both the opening and closing ceremonies took place in the stadium. The special athletes were joined by many celebrities, including news correspondent Maria Shriver, the late Dick Sargent of television's "Bewitched," and Don Johnson, known for his role on TV's "Miami Vice."

6. **A**cademic achievement was center stage in the stadium when the University conducted its annual spring commencement exercises there.

7. Getting an opportunity to share in the special memories of Notre Dame Stadium is the reward awaiting members of the teams playing in the University's annual interhall football championships. Here contestants in a recent match for the women's interhall title congratulate each other after a good game.

8. Notre Dame was the site for the 1987 International Summer Special Olympics Games. Hundreds of special athletes joined thousands of volunteers, sponsors, coaches, and spectators for the opening and closing ceremonies held in the stadium.

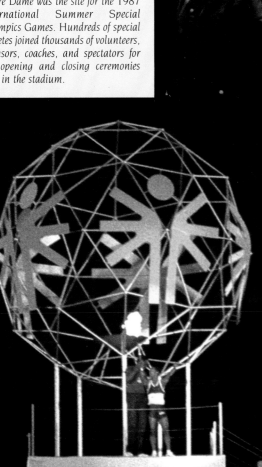

The new stadium at Notre Dame in 1930 meant a lot to the media as the reporters no longer would have to stand in the rain, snow, wind, or sleet that is an inevitable and inescapable part of South Bend weather during football season. Now there would be a glass-enclosed press box with stacked viewing rows to accommodate 264 writers. Each sports writer was allotted 24 inches of counter with which to do his job. Provisions were also made for photographers, with a photo deck situated just above the working press area. On the roof were the broadcasting and coaches boxes and, later, several modest suites for University officials and their guests.

The press box rose 60 feet from the ground and stretched 142 feet, noted *Scholastic Magazine*. It spread between the 25-yard lines on the west side of the stadium. *The South Bend News-Times* reported on November 29, 1937, that "the press box above the Notre Dame Stadium is the largest of its kind in the country" and "sports writers agree that it has more 'elbow room' than any other football press box." (By 1996, Notre Dame's press box was among the smallest in major college football. The stadium's new press box is four times as large.)

One restriction in the press box during the early years was the prohibition of women. Although an exception was made—once—even the first season, when Mrs. Knute Rockne passed through the press box en route to a radio booth for a halftime interview.

Two decades later the denizens of the press box were strictly male, as reflected in a 1948 letter written by Charlie Callahan, the University's sports information director, who observed of the press box's "modernity": "Among the usual conveniences is a large size men's room."

Callahan added, "A snack bar is located in the back of the press box... Cokes, coffee, and hot dogs are furnished free at all times and distributed to the seat holders and those in the radio booths at halftime."

Today, the seat holders help themselves, but the tradition of "free eats" continues for members of the media covering ND football.

1. New York Times *sports writer and columnist Walter "Red" Smith was a 1927 graduate of Notre Dame. He often returned to his alma mater to cover Fighting Irish football. Smith won the Pulitzer Prize for commentary in 1976. He died in 1982. The University sponsors the annual Red Smith Lecture Series and a scholarship in his honor.*

IOWA
NOVEMBER 19, 1960
Press Box
ROOF
BOOTH
5

NO WOMEN
OR CHILDREN
PERMITTED IN
PRESS BOX

AMERICAN TICKET CORP.
NEAR, CHICAGO ILLS, C   77

ADMIT
ONE
PRESS GATE

S tadium announcer  Mike Collins loves the hot dogs:

"The hot dogs they served in the [old] press box were the best hot dogs in sports," Collins claims. "I don't usually eat them anywhere else, but I'd eat three of those a game. I'm just hoping that whoever had the press box concession before is back when the new one opens."

Collins, a 1967 graduate of Notre Dame, has announced the games in the stadium for 16 years. He is best known in the South Bend community as a veteran journalist and broadcaster, currently serving as managing editor of news at WSBT-TV.

Of all he has seen in the stadium as a student and announcer, two games stand out in Collins' mind: Miami in 1988 and Florida State in 1993.

"The passions and emotions were so great," Collins recalls. "There was so much excitement and so much noise, and I'm doing my best trying to be a professional PA announcer."

In an effort to keep himself under control, Collins says he nearly did the second halves of each of those games standing up.

"When that Florida State game was over," Collins says, reliving the moment, "I gave over my headset and just screamed my head off. Sometimes, you have to be just a fan."

Collins was preceded in the PA booth by Frank Crosiar, who announced the games from 1948 to 1981. He never missed one of the 170 games during those years. Neither to date has Collins missed any of his 86 opportunities to call the action for the Irish faithful in the stands.

"THERE HAVE BEEN TIMES WHEN YOU WALK AROUND THE INSIDE OF THE STADIUM AND YOU'LL HEAR A DOOR CLOSE BEHIND YOU... AND THERE'S NO ONE THERE TO CLOSE THE DOOR.

"I'VE BEEN IN THERE EARLY IN THE MORNING AND BECAUSE THE STADIUM IS SO OLD THERE ARE CREAKS. THE WOOD AND THE BRICK AND THE TEMPERATURE EXPANSION AND THINGS LIKE THAT...THINGS YOU WOULDN'T NORMALLY HEAR IN A STADIUM THAT SIZE THAT WAS BUILT, SAY, IN 1950. YOU WALK AROUND DOWN THERE UNDERNEATH AND IT CAN GET A LITTLE SPOOKY."

Jeff Jeffers, Sports Director, WNDU-TV

1. "Win one for the Gipper...," perhaps the most famous quote from all of sports, introduced in the 1940 theatrical film release "Knute Rockne, All American" (here with Pat O'Brien, as Rockne, and future television "Superman" George Reeves) and made a lexicon of modern American politics by former President Ronald Reagan, who played ill-starred Notre Dame halfback George Gipp in the movie. The plaque with Gipp's dying words still hangs in the varsity locker room as an inspiration to the latest generation of Fighting Irish players.

2. Notre Dame players used to draw their equipment from an issue room in the stadium until more modern facilities opened in the Joyce Center, which also is closer to the team's practice fields to the east. However, enlarged team spaces in the renovated stadium has meant a partial return to the old way. Today's team equips and dresses for practice, as well as games, in the stadium locker room.

3. The inner sanctum of the fanfare and frenzy that so often is Notre Dame football. For all the shouting and cheering that takes place in the stands outside, inside the varsity locker room on game day the atmosphere is unusually quiet and composed.

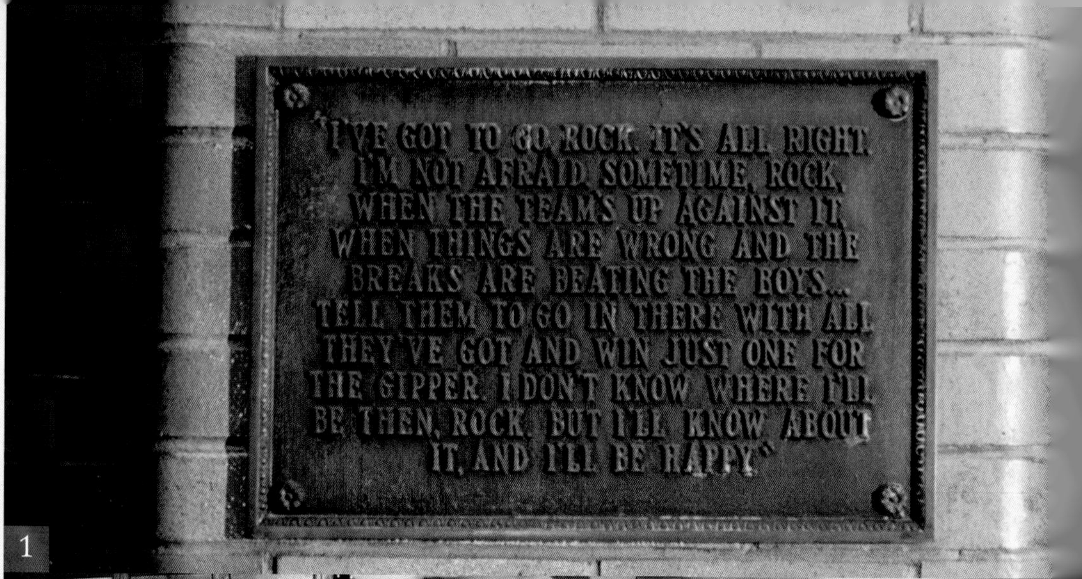

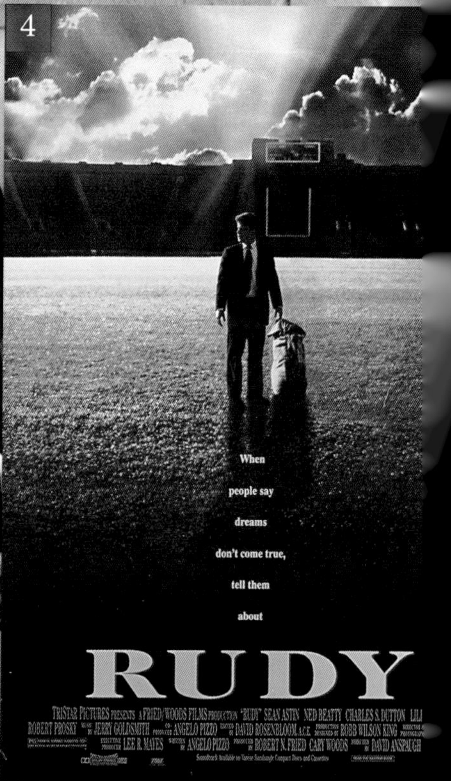

When people say dreams don't come true, tell them about

RUDY

NOTRE DAME
FIGHTING IRISH
NATIONAL
CHAMPIONS

1924 10-0-0
1929 9-0-0
1930 10-0-0
1943 9-1-0
1946 8-0-1
1947 9-0-0
1949 10-0-0
1966 9-0-1
1973 11-0-0
1977 11-1-0
1988 12-0-0

PLAY LIKE
A CHAMPION
TODAY

4. *(opposite page)* The 1993 TriStar Pictures release RUDY is the only other major motion picture actually filmed on the Notre Dame campus. The promotional poster for the movie is a shot of actor Sean Astin— "Rudy"—standing in the original Notre Dame Stadium.

5. Time tunnel—nearly four generations of Irish players have emerged from this tunnel into Notre Dame football history. A chance to run through the tunnel onto the field at Notre Dame Stadium is considered the ultimate goal of many top high school players across the country.

6. A last reminder to "Play Like a Champion" waits for Notre Dame players at the bottom of the stairs leading from the varsity locker room to the tunnel at the north end of the stadium. Tradition is for every player to touch the sign before taking the field. Also intended to impress the players is a tally of Notre Dame's unprecedented 11 national championship-winning seasons.

M any talented players have thrilled football fans on Saturday afternoons at Notre Dame Stadium during its 67-year history. Among them, the University's seven Heisman Trophy winners, in chronological order: Angelo Bertelli (1943), John Lujack ('47), Leon Hart ('49), John Lattner ('53), Paul Hornung ('56), John Huarte ('64), and Tim Brown ('87).

As every true Notre Dame fan knows and is quick to boast, no other school can claim as many recipients of college football's highest accolade.

Between 1930 and the end of the 1996 season, 324 games were played on the stadium's grass. Every fan can recall his or her favorite "Notre Dame moment," and for many it is the final play of the Notre Dame v. Michigan game on Sept. 20, 1980.

The Irish were trailing 27-26, and time was running out. Notre Dame started on its own 20-yard line and moved the ball 46 yards in 41 seconds. Now with only four ticks left on the clock, there was time for one last snap. It would be a field goal, of course. A 51-yard field goal—against the wind—and all eyes focused on the kicker, Harry Oliver. He had never kicked a ball longer than 38 yards in his career. Earlier in the same game he had missed an extra point after a touchdown.

The ball was snapped, set, and the kick was made. As the pigskin sailed through the uprights, the final gun sounded. Notre Dame defeated the Wolverines, 29-27. The crowd went wild. Tim Koegel, who held the ball for the game-winning kick, said, "You know, just as I placed the ball down, the wind died down...almost stopped. I knew then we'd make it."

Unlike the last "change of venue" for Notre Dame football, none of the old stadium field was kept to sow luck in the new.

"The [old] field was so worn out that it wouldn't stay together," says Craig Rudell, owner of Magic Carpet Turf Farms in Buchanan Township, Michigan, where the Merion blue grass for the new field was seeded 15 months before being laid on the floor of Notre Dame Stadium. Eighty thousand square feet of new sod was cut in rolls 42 inches wide and 90 feet long; each roll covered about 30 square yards, minimizing seams in the field. The field itself was lowered only nine inches during the renovation, owing mostly to elimination of a crown previously needed for drainage.

1. Derrick Mayes (1) making one of his numerous touchdown catches as a split end for Notre Dame. When he graduated, Mayes was the Irish career leader in receiving yards (2,512) and touchdown receptions (22).

2. Notre Dame's seven Heisman Trophy winners, who galloped into college football history across the gridiron of Notre Dame Stadium. From left to right, top: Angelo Bertelli (1943), John Lujack ('47), Leon Hart ('49), John Lattner ('53); bottom: Paul Hornung ('56), John Huarte ('64), and Tim Brown ('87).

3. Four of Notre Dame's Heisman winners pose with Head Coach Bob Davie during a preseason visit to the expanded Notre Dame Stadium. From left are Leon Hart, John Lujack, Coach Davie, Paul Hornung, and John Huarte. Also, at right, is former Notre Dame player Creighton Miller, a consensus All-American for the Irish in 1943.

4. Harry Oliver launches a 51-yard field goal—against the wind—to defeat Michigan 29-27, Sept. 20, 1980. Tim Koegel was the holder for Oliver, whose longest previous field goal was 38 yards. For many Fighting Irish fans, it is the definitive "Notre Dame moment."

esides the football players, coaches, officials, cheerleaders, and camera people on the field, there's another group on the sidelines at every Notre Dame home game: the Band of the Fighting Irish and the Irish Guard (left).

The young men of the Guard wear Irish kilts of Notre Dame plaid. Its gold and blue represent the University's colors, and green is intermixed for an Irish touch. The Guards' jackets are papal red. With their tall hats made of bearskin, Guard members stand more than eight feet tall. The criteria for membership in the Irish Guard are marching ability, appearance, spirit, and a minimum height of 6'2".

Established in 1845, the Band of the Fighting Irish is the oldest university marching band in America. The band has attended every home game since football began at the University in 1887. Today there are more than 300 musicians in the band, averaging about 75 per class.

"Going through the tunnel is still the biggest thrill," says Luther Snavely, band director for ten years. Of the freshmen who march through the tunnel for their first game, Snavely says: "There are very few of them that ever play a note that first game. They'll be so excited. They'll be nervous and will be soaking it all up."

The band practices 90 minutes a day, Monday through Friday, preparing for a halftime program that runs about seven and a half minutes.

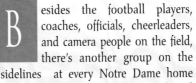

5. As integral to any football game in Notre Dame Stadium as the football players, the Band of the Fighting Irish is the oldest college marching band in the country. Although not always the largest, as reflected in the archival photo at right, the band has never failed to contribute its energy to the Irish cause at every home game since football began at Notre Dame in 1887. Today, the band includes more than 300 members.

In 1930, when this aerial shot of campus was taken, Herbert Hoover was President, the Great Depression had just begun, and Notre Dame was still a small Catholic men's college with fewer than 3,000 students. Its new stadium, however, could seat 60,000 and did, routinely, through the glory days of the 1940s under Coach Frank Leahy.

When Rev. Theodore Hesburgh, CSC, took over as University president in 1952, he remarked as to how Notre Dame had a rather modest physical plant, a not particularly distinguished faculty, an "average" student body, and the No. 1 football team in the nation. Father Hesburgh joked—and not without serious consideration— that his goal was to build a University that the football team could be proud of. The success of Hesburgh and current University President Rev. Edward A. "Monk" Malloy, CSC, in achieving that goal during the intervening 45 years is reflected in the succeeding pages (overleaf).

Notre Dame today (overleaf) is a much larger and different place than the one pictured left. Roughly 10,500 undergraduate, graduate, and professional students now populate campus. They represent all 50 states and more than 80 foreign countries, making Notre Dame America's most national university. Also, approximately 45 percent of today's student body is female, women having been admitted to the University's previously all-male undergraduate curriculum in 1972.

A number of independent reviews in recent years consistently ranked Notre Dame among the top 20 premier universities in the nation. Its leadership extends from traditional areas of scholarly expertise like theology and philosophy to nuclear physics, environmental science, Medieval studies, electrical and chemical engineering, accounting, computer technology, classic design, biogenetic research, ethics, and the law, as well as community service.

LEAHY

FRANK LEAHY (1941-43, '46-53)
WHILE COACHING THE IRISH, LEAHY HAD SIX UNDEFEATED SEASONS AND WON FOUR NATIONAL CHAMPIONSHIPS (1943, '46, '47, '49). LEAHY LEFT HIS COACHING POST IN 1944-45 TO SERVE IN THE NAVY DURING WORLD WAR II.

"WE ARE SEARCHING FOR PERFECTION IN FOOTBALL, THE SAME WAY WE SEEK PERFECTION IN EVERYTHING WE DO AT NOTRE DAME. THE FOOTBALL TEAM IS A SYMBOL OF WHAT THE ENTIRE UNIVERSITY SHOULD BE LIKE. PERFECTION IS THE GOAL." — FRANK LEAHY

ARA

ARA PARSEGHIAN (1964-74)
DURING THE ERA OF ARA, NOTRE DAME WON THREE NATIONAL CHAMPIONSHIPS: THE MACARTHUR BOWL FROM THE NATIONAL FOOTBALL FOUNDATION AND HALL OF FAME IN 1964, THEN IN '66 AND '73 IN POLLS BY SPORTSWRITERS AND BROADCASTERS.

"THE FIRST DAY I CAME ONTO THE CAMPUS AND DROVE UP THE AVENUE THAT TAKES YOU TO THE GOLDEN DOME, A CHARGE WENT UP MY BACK. I REMEMBERED WHAT ROCKNE HAD DONE AND WHAT LEAHY HAD DONE, AND I KNEW WHAT I WAS RESPONSIBLE FOR." — ARA PARSEGHIAN

DEVINE

DAN DEVINE (1975-80)
DEVINE LED THE IRISH TO ANOTHER NATIONAL CHAMPIONSHIP IN 1977 BEATING THEN-NUMBER ONE RANKED TEXAS 38-10 IN THE COTTON BOWL. THE LONGHORNS WERE THE ONLY OTHER UNDEFEATED COLLEGE TEAM UNTIL THEY MET THE IRISH.

"IT SEEMS THAT EVERYWHERE IT'S SAID THAT PEOPLE ARE WHAT MAKE NOTRE DAME SUCH A GREAT PLACE. I COULDN'T AGREE MORE. FROM FATHERS HESBURGH AND JOYCE DOWN THROUGH THE FACULTY AND ATHLETIC ADMINISTRATION TO THE STUDENTS THEMSELVES, NOTRE DAME PEOPLE ARE SPECIAL IN THEIR OWN WAY." — DAN DEVINE

LOU

LOU HOLTZ (1986-96)
IN THE 1988 FIESTA BOWL, NOTRE DAME BEAT NUMBER ONE RANKED AND UNDEFEATED WEST VIRGINIA TO WIN ITS ELEVENTH NATIONAL CHAMPIONSHIP. HOLTZ'S TEAMS PLAYED IN POSTSEASON BOWL GAMES FOR NINE CONSECUTIVE YEARS (BEGINNING IN 1987), A NOTRE DAME RECORD. HIS THOUGHTS ON THE RENOVATED STADIUM: *"I'M EXCITED BECAUSE MORE PEOPLE WILL HAVE THE OPPORTUNITY TO EXPERIENCE A NOTRE DAME WEEKEND. THIS ISN'T ABOUT FOOTBALL. THIS IS ABOUT ENABLING MORE FAMILY, FRIENDS, AND ASSOCIATES TO COME TO THE CAMPUS AND SEE THINGS LIKE THE GROTTO, SACRED HEART, THE HESBURGH LIBRARY AND THE GOLDEN DOME, AS WELL AS NOTRE DAME STADIUM."*

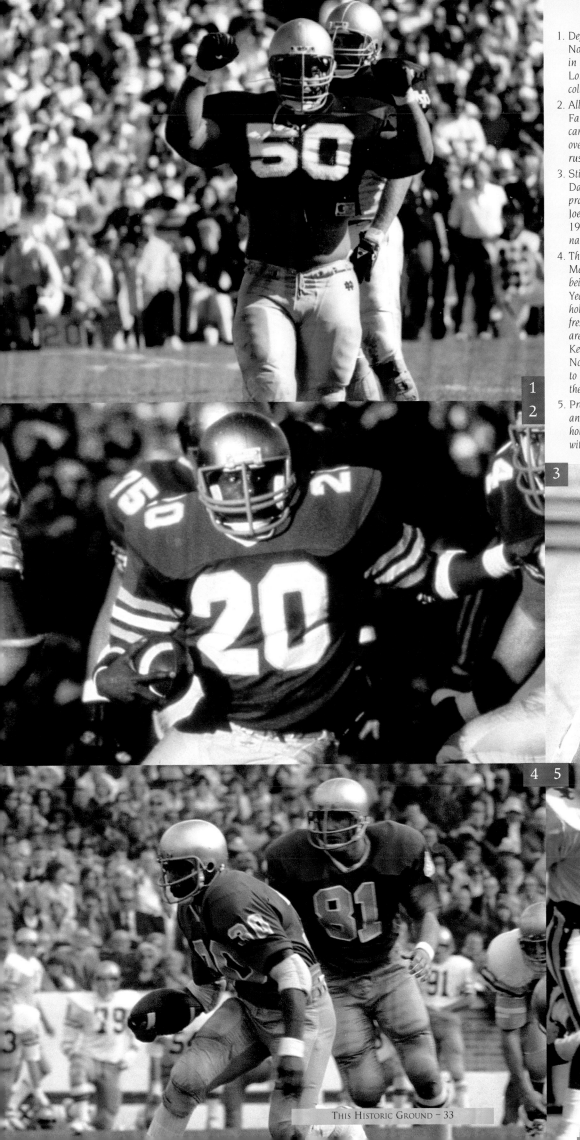

1. Defensive tackle Chris Zorich helped lead Notre Dame to its last national championship in 1988; two years later he'd win the Lombardi Award as the nation's outstanding college lineman.

2. Allen Pinkett (#20), playing for Coach Jerry Faust, established Notre Dame records for career yards rushing (4,131), career games over 100 yards rushing (21), and career rushing touchdowns (49).

3. Still the subject of more queries to Notre Dame's Sports Information office than practically any other Fighting Irish player, Joe Montana led Coach Dan Devine's 1977 Notre Dame squad to yet another national title.

4. Three-time All-America tight end Ken MacAfee (#81) concluded his Irish career by being named the Walter Camp Player of the Year in 1977. Jerome Heavens (#30) still holds Notre Dame's rushing record for a freshman (756 yards in 1975). Both players are notable here, as well, for wearing the Kelly green jerseys sometimes employed by Notre Dame coaches as a "secret weapon" to motivate Irish players and intimidate the opposition.

5. Probably the fastest man ever to wear the gold and blue, Raghib Ismail (1989-90) also holds Notre Dame's 100 meter dash record with a time of 10.2 seconds.

It held on longer than most. Because tradition runs deeper here than almost anywhere. But, by the 1990s, Notre Dame Stadium was showing the signs of age after more than six decades of service. Even the most conservative Fighting Irish fan believed the time had come to bring the stadium from the era of leather helmets and the full house backfield into the modern day.

Also by the '90s, the ranks of Notre Dame alumni—already more than 100,000 strong—were growing by more than 2,000 graduates a year. The demand for football tickets was increasing proportionately. Since the run of consecutive stadium sellouts (except for a 1973 Thanksgiving Day game against Air Force) began in 1966, the University has used a lottery system for distributing football tickets to alumni. At the start of the 1996 season, the chances of any contributing alum receiving tickets to any Notre Dame home game had narrowed to less than 50-50.

In September 1991, the Notre Dame National Alumni Board of Directors again officially asked the University administration to consider expanding the stadium.

"We believe we have a legitimate need," said Alumni Association Executive Director Charles F. Lennon, Jr., who found a sympathetic listener in Notre Dame Board of Trustees Chairman Andrew J. McKenna.

"Alumni, in particular, have become increasingly frustrated by the lack of opportunities to return to campus for football games," McKenna reported to the board. What was needed, he added, "was a plan of expansion which would not interfere with the rapid academic advancements being made by the University and which, in fact, would be capable of contributing to [its] academic and student life needs."

As fate would have it, the University in 1991-92 was involved in a comprehensive review of all of its anticipated needs going into the next century. In his 1993 final report of the Colloquy for the Year 2000, Notre Dame President Rev. Edward A. Malloy, CSC, included expansion of the stadium as one of 43 recommendations he submitted to the Board of Trustees.

However, before any expansion was approved, two criteria had to be met: first, it could not divert financial resources from any other University priority. Second, the financial *benefits* of any expansion would be applied to the educational mission at Notre Dame. Similarly, proceeds from Notre Dame's NBC television contract are used to help provide financial aid to deserving students in need.

May 6, 1994: the Notre Dame Board of Trustees approves a plan to expand the stadium by roughly 21,000 seats. The decision is the culmination of a long and comprehensive study of the options to either renovate and expand, or build anew. (The notion of building a new stadium never gets far: "I don't want to be remembered in history as the man who tore down 'The House That Rockne Built,'" remarks Rev. E. William Beauchamp, CSC, who as executive vice president of the University is chair of the Faculty Board on Athletics.)

Enlarging an existing stadium—especially one 65 years old—is no simple task, however. It requires careful planning, in this case, by Ellerbe Becket Architects of Kansas City, MO. The same firm also designed the Joyce Athletic and Convocation Center (1968) on campus and, more recently, the Olympic Stadium in Atlanta.

Groundbreaking for the stadium renovation and expansion took place on November 6, 1995, less than 48 hours after the Irish finished their home game schedule that year. The renovated stadium would debut on September 6, 1997, exactly 22 months after the first shovels of dirt are turned.

1. University Board of Trustees Chairman Andrew J. McKenna and Notre Dame Executive Vice President Rev. E. William Beauchamp, CSC, announce at a press conference in May 1994 that the University will expand Notre Dame Stadium by some 21,000 seats, thereby elating thousands of Notre Dame alumni grown increasingly desperate for tickets during the sellout decades of the 1970s, '80s, and '90s.

2. Wasting no time, work on the stadium renovation and expansion began immediately after the final home game of the 1995 season. In this shot of the north facade taken the morning of the official groundbreaking just two days later, November 6, one can see that some of the cap stones above the exterior brick work (right) already have been removed.

3. Doing the honors at the official groundbreaking ceremonies for the stadium expansion were, from left, Notre Dame Alumni Association Executive Director Charles F. Lennon, Jr.; Head Coach Lou Holtz; former Irish player and current Notre Dame Director of Athletics Michael Wadsworth; University Executive Vice President Rev. E. William Beauchamp, CSC; student body vice president Dennis McCarthy; and president Jonathan Patrick.

4. Media gather for the groundbreaking, an event that made sports page headlines from coast to coast. Father Beauchamp tells South Bend sportscaster Jack Nolan that the expansion project will cost approximately $50 million and that it will be paid for with the additional revenue generated from 21,000 new seats. He adds that the University's academic and student life programs will be the long-term beneficiaries of the new dollars.

5. Construction of the stadium's enlarged bowl begins at the stadium's north end. The existing parapet around the top of the old stadium ring must be removed in order to eventually join the old and new sections of the building.

1. A little off the top... The block cap stones are removed early in the demolition phase of the stadium project. Unlike many of the bricks from the old stadium that were sold to Notre Dame alumni, fans, and collectors, these blocks were broken and thrown away. But, many chunks were scooped up by casual passersby during the first days of the project, before a security fence was erected around the site.

2. The new exterior wall of the stadium will extend 85 feet out from the shell of the original structure, meaning all of the trees that surround the stadium—and, in some cases, had grown above its rim—are cut down. However, allowances are made in plans for the expanded stadium (see opposite page) to replace the trees removed many times over.

3. Three of the original 18 gates into Notre Dame Stadium in a photograph that also preserves some of the other architectural features of the first structure, including the rich texture of the brick work. In the years before the stadium's expansion, other campus buildings moved into close proximity and the nature of "Notre Dame brick" changed. Brick on the new exterior walls of the stadium is of the lighter shade used in the construction of neighboring DeBartolo Hall and the College of Business Administration building.

4. The architects' expectation of what the expanded Notre Dame Stadium would look like. As seen in a later chapter, the real thing turned out with very few changes from this artist rendering.

5. "Can you still see Jesus?"... That was the question on the minds of many Notre Dame fans when confronting the impact of the stadium expansion on the view of the "Word of Life" mural—"Touchdown Jesus"—on Hesburgh Library, just a glance up from the stadium's north end zone. This shot was taken early in the construction from about row 40 and shows the degree of obscurity caused by the stadium's new upper ring.

1 2

3

1. Nearly seven decades of midwestern winters took a heavy toll on the original stadium's concrete. A large portion of the renovation phase of the stadium project was dedicated to replacing deteriorated sections of the lower bowl. Restoration workers detected areas needing replacement by tapping with a hammer practically every square inch of concrete in the original structure.

2. What was the varsity locker room becomes a metal shop in this photograph. Renovation of the locker room will roughly double its size. New equipment, office, and training areas also are added. Six spectator entrances at the north end of the bowl, above the locker room, must be raised to create the necessary space.

3. From the outset, the intent was to preserve as much of the original Notre Dame Stadium as possible. Virtually none of the load of the new stands will bear on the 1930 construction. Here the first support pillars for the upper bowl are put in place. In the background are two other recent University buildings, DeBartolo Hall and the College of Business Administration.

4

4. The past meets the present in this shot as demolition of the original parapet is completed. The ring will be transformed into a walkway serving the new stands above and providing more areas for handicapped seating.

1. Duplicating a building method used in the original construction, concrete sections used in the stadium's expansion were preformed off-site and then brought in and erected. Sixty-three hundred separate pieces of precast concrete were required to build the stadium's enlarged bowl and new upper and lower concourses, the lightest weighing several hundred pounds and the heaviest more than 40 tons.

2. Even with modern machinery, like the 230-ton crane shown at right, assembling the many intricate parts of the stadium addition took the better part of eight months, or twice as long as the time it took to put up the original building. The quality and fine tolerances of the materials used, however, required much time-consuming precision for their installation.

3. At one time as many as 300 construction workers clambered about the stadium construction site, contributing to the as many as 800 workers on campus during the summer of 1996 when the University also was in the process of building four new residence halls, starting a restoration of the Main Building, renovating the School of Architecture's Bond Hall, and managing many smaller projects. At the time, the value of Notre Dame building projects underway exceeded $125 million.

4. The final section of precast concrete is hoisted into place at the south end of expanded Notre Dame Stadium. Twenty-six rows have been added to The House That Rockne Built, and those in the top row now sit almost 85 feet above street level. Still, early visitors to the enlarged stadium report views of the field from up high are pretty good, and views of the campus from some sections are even better.

5. Work continues into the cold weather months of 1996-97. Here, stone masons bundled against Mother Nature's version of Hoosier hospitality install precast atop one of the stadium's four new stairwells.

6. As happened with the original stadium, construction workers from across America converged on Notre Dame for a chance to work on the expansion project. Many expressed personal pride at being able to contribute to the re-creation of what some see as the closest thing in America to a national monument to college athletics...one that should last, at least, another 67 years.

A peculiar mix of the old and the new is reflected in this series of photographs, which also begins to suggest the relative scales of the old and new stadiums. This is particularly true of the stadium's new press box, which clearly dwarfs its predecessor. Also seen for the first time are the permanent lights installed on the press box and at the four corners of the stadium for late fall games extending into twilight. They were actually put to use for the last two games of the 1996 season. Early in the lights discussion, Notre Dame Executive Vice President Rev. E. William Beauchamp, CSC, reiterated the University's position that there will be no night games at Notre Dame Stadium.

In the photograph at bottom, the famous turf of the original field is gone. Unlike when the Fighting Irish moved into the stadium in 1930 and a piece of old Cartier Field was sown into the new playing surface to help ensure continuation of Notre Dame's winning tradition, none of the stadium field in 1995 was fit to make a similar transfer. Also shown here is, perhaps, the singular item of the stadium left untouched during the entire renovation and expansion project...the flag pole.

The press box was one of the more highly anticipated features of the new stadium. Similar to a design at Brigham Young University, Notre Dame's Jim and Marilyn Fitzgerald Family Sports and Communications Center, as the press box is known, includes separate levels for the working (print) press, and for radio and television broadcast, as well as a University level for official and informal entertaining.

The first game "under the lights" at Notre Dame Stadium occurred in September 1982 vs. Michigan. Temporary lights were brought in to accommodate a nationwide, prime-time broadcast of the Irish-Wolverines match up. With the inception of Notre Dame's television contract with NBC, the University has guaranteed continuation of national broadcast coverage of the Fighting Irish, while establishing a standard (1:30 p.m. EST) time for kickoff.

1. "Can you still see Jesus?"... Perhaps not as well from the stands, anymore, but the view from the new upper concourse is impressive in its own right. A walk around the upper concourse is a highlight of the new Notre Dame Stadium, providing an open-air, 360-degree tour of the University's campus, long regarded as among the most picturesque in the country.

2. Improving access to the stadium for the disabled was a leading objective of the expanded stadium's designers. Four ramps—two each at the north and south ends of the stadium—help make the upper reaches of the new structure accessible to persons in wheelchairs. The new stadium also includes three elevators (with allowances for a fourth), in place of the single lift that once served the building and traveled back and forth only to the press box.

3. While hundreds of bricks from the original stadium found their way to Notre Dame alumni, fans, and collectors, more than 22,000 were recycled during the renovation and expansion. Ten new "gates" were cut in the old stadium's facade (4 opposite), now the inside wall of the lower concourse, and many of the bricks were reused in finishing around the new openings. Others were recycled as a planter that now occupies the space behind the team benches on the east and west sides of the field. The planter takes the place of the stadium's original rows 1 and 2; spectators in those lowest seats often had their view blocked by the players on the sidelines just in front of them.

4

5

5. Two workers give dimension to the stadium's new lower concourse. An interior view of one of the new pedestrian ramps, located right, has an almost honeycomb look, creating a nice architectural display of shadows and light. In other places, meanwhile 6, looking out from the ramps offers neatly framed pictures of parts of the Notre Dame campus, in this case, Decio Faculty Hall and Hesburgh Library.

7. Welcome to new Notre Dame Stadium...the view greeting fans entering the upper seating sections, many of them new Fighting Irish football ticket holders. Of the approximately 21,000 seats added, 16,000 were apportioned to Notre Dame alumni, increasing by 100 percent the total seats available to alumni at each home game. The University also was able to nearly double the number of tickets available to faculty and staff.

6
7

(opposite) A dramatic entrance...the south entrance to expanded Notre Dame Stadium, striking even before the gold leaf is added to the title above the door. Seen in the foreground is the south loop of Moose Krause Drive, which encircles the new stadium and is named in honor of the late Edward W. "Moose" Krause, long-time Notre Dame director of athletics.

1. Two million bricks were used in the stadium's original construction in 1930. Even though the expansion's outer wall is larger in area than the original exterior, more architectural precast is featured in its design and fewer than 620,000 bricks are used for the stadium's new facade.

2. Putting on a good face...brick masons about halfway through their work on the stadium's east side. The scaffolds in use actually "climb" their support pillars as each level of the job is completed.

1. Replacing weathered redwood seating in the original bowl was only part of the renovation phase of the stadium project...maybe the smallest part. While repairing deteriorated sections of the original concrete risers, the contractors also took the opportunity to install all new metal stanchions for the bleachers. That meant burning out the anchor bolts used for the old stanchions—all 44,000 of them! The job was done, one by one, by just two workers using blowtorches **2**.

3. The fixed stadium seating that replaced the (in)famous green folding chairs in the preferred seating sections of the stadium. Visible in the middle of the picture is the sidelines-long planter that replaced rows 1 and 2 of the original stadium. The planter raises the lowest rows above the level of the players in front of them on game day, improving the sight lines of the fans in those seats.

(opposite) Though now among the tallest buildings on campus, the stadium is still humbled by the stature—actual as well as symbolic—of the two most prominent structures at Notre Dame, the spire of the Basilica of the Sacred Heart and the golden-domed Main Building.

1. The finishing touches are applied to the new Notre Dame Stadium. Despite a slowdown of the construction made necessary by the Fighting Irish continuing to play in the facility during the 1996 season **2**, the project is completed on time. The finished product becomes the 15th largest college football stadium (from 44th) in America, and one of the most modern. All that remains (opposite) is the first arrival of 80,000 fans for the Rededication Game against Georgia Tech on Sept. 6, 1997.

SECTION FOUR:
HOUSE REDEDICATED

Dawn of a new era... the sun rises on a fresh chapter in the storied history of Notre Dame Stadium and Fighting Irish football, September 6, 1997.

"Football history will be made today...,"

University President Rev. Charles L. O'Donnell, CSC, at the original dedication of Notre Dame Stadium October 11, 1930

T he excitement and anticipation that has surrounded every Fighting Irish home game since the original Notre Dame Stadium opened in 1930 increased exponentially in 1997. As football season approached, it was not only a new team, but also a new head coach and the dedication of a renewed stadium that heightened expectations for a day so many had waited for so long.

Still, another 67 years into the history of Notre Dame Stadium, in the year 2064, historians may note only that the day was Sept. 6. The opponent was Georgia Tech. The weather was sunny and warm. The home team won.

Lost in the echoes of more recent cheers will be the words that proclaimed the historic event, the reopening of the most famous college athletic venue in America.

Unlikely to be remembered, the thunder of nearly 80,000 fans as the Fighting Irish took to their new field through a cordon of former Notre Dame players, each a contributor to the legendary history embedded in the surrounding walls. Forgotten, too, a sense of the crest and fall and crest again of emotions as the Irish battled from behind to pull out a victory in the final few minutes of play, another tally in the long "W" column of Notre Dame football.

What is certain to endure, however, is the mystique that creates itself around such moments, that connects five generations of alumni, family, and fans one to another, that revels in an already rich tradition, that will only become more historic in the years ahead... the spirit of Notre Dame.

"If you could find a way to bottle the Notre Dame spirit, you could light up the universe..."
—Joe Theisman
Notre Dame quarterback 1968-70

1. University Executive Vice President Rev. E. William Beauchamp, CSC, greets the morning television audience watching the official ribbon cutting ceremonies for expanded Notre Dame Stadium. Behind Fr. Beauchamp are, from left, Director of Athletics Michael Wadsworth, University President Rev. Edward A. Malloy, CSC, Chuck Lennon, executive director of the Notre Dame Alumni Association, and Associate Director of Athletics Bubba Cunningham.

2. Let the games begin...the gates of Notre Dame Stadium are officially opened to the more than 80,000 fans who will eventually file through the turnstiles to see the Fighting Irish take on Georgia Tech in the first game inside the restored and enlarged landmark.

3

4 5

3. For the first time, Notre Dame Stadium will host more than 80,000 fans for a Fighting Irish football game. The day was blessed with sunshine and warm temperatures as seen in this aerial shot, that also compares with the architect's rendering on p. 37 to show the accuracy with which the stadium's builders executed the construction plan.

4. Notre Dame President Rev. Edward A. Malloy, CSC, offers words of welcome, thanks, and praise during pre-game activities inside the stadium. Fr. Malloy included expansion of the stadium among his 43 recommendations in the final report of the Colloquy for the Year 2000, thus setting in motion the final steps toward actually increasing the size of "The House That Rockne Built." Also pictured are Mr. and Mrs. Terrance J. McGlinn, benefactors of another new building on campus, McGlinn Hall, one of four new residence halls located on West Quad.

5. The Band of the Fighting Irish celebrates the stadium's grand re-opening by debuting something new of its own, a routine spelling out the most renowned university moniker in America.

(opposite) The Notre Dame student section provides the backdrop for this photo of kickoff in the new stadium. Most of the students wear "the shirt," a tradition at the first home game of each season. A fundraising effort, sales of "the shirt" have raised a million dollars for charity during the past seven years.

1. Tailback Autry Denson goes into the Notre Dame record books as the player to score the first touchdown in the new stadium, staking the Irish to an early lead against Georgia Tech, which battles back to knot the score 10-10 at halftime.

2. Junior defensive back Benny Guilbeaux snuffs a Georgia Tech scoring drive at the start of the third quarter by intercepting this pass attempt in the end zone. Both teams go scoreless in the quarter. But, on the first play of the fourth quarter, Georgia Tech kicks a field goal to take the lead 13-10.

3. Quarterback Ron Powlus celebrates Notre Dame's game-winning drive in the closing moments of the game, culminated by Autry Denson's one-yard touchdown plunge 4 with just 2:33 remaining. The Fighting Irish inaugurate the new stadium with a 17-13 victory.

PHOTOGRAPHS

p. 4, Linda Dunn, pp. 6-7, courtesy University Archives (5), Notre Dame Monogram Club Heritage Collection (1)
p. 8, Linda Dunn (2), University Archives (3), Notre Dame Photographic Collection (1), p. 9, Bruce Harlan (2),
University Archives (1), pp. 10-11, courtesy Notre Dame Sports Information (4), University Archives (3), p. 12, Linda
Dunn (3), University Archives (4), p. 13, Linda Dunn (1), Bruce Harlan (1), p. 14, ND Sports Information (2), p. 15
Chuck Linster (1), p. 16, Bruce Harlan (4), p. 17, Christopher Broadhurst (6), St. Kathleen Beaty (1), University
Archives (1), p. 18, ND Photographic Collection (1), ND Sports Information (4), p. 19, Michael Benson (1), p. 20,
Michael Benson (1), ND Photographic Collection (2), p. 21, Michael Benson (1), p. 22, ND Photographic Collection
(8), p. 23, John Bingham (2), University Archives (2), pp. 24-27, University Archives, pp. 28-31, Burke, Chris Lewis &
Mike Young, p. 34, Linda Dunn (1), Bruce Harlan (3), University Archives (3), p. 35, ND Sports Information (5),
p. 39, courtesy Blanke Racket Archives (1), p. 42, Bruce Harlan (1), pp. 58-65, Chris Lewis & Mike Young, p. 69, Bill
Steinmetz (1), back cover, Bill Steinmetz (1).